COVID-22

COVID-22
CS HUGHES

MAXIMUM
FELIX MEDIA

COVID-22
ISBN: 9780648589570
COPYRIGHT

C S HUGHES

FIRST PUBLISHED JUNE 2020

By

MAXIMUM FELIX MEDIA
PO BOX 440
KORUMBURRA
VIC 3950
AUSTRALIA

ALL RIGHTS RESERVED.

This is a work of imagination. Any resemblance to situations, events, institutions, entities, places or persons living or dead is purely coincidental.

**MAXIMUM
FELIX MEDIA**

poetry is an affliction

God is **not** a **vaccine**.

Quite alone
I will bend like triumph
To her laurels

Here, life has become
A struggle with silence
The band strikes up
In defiance or resignation
To that shimmering
Sunfall cacophony
Cymbal bright and
Dying
A last bombastic stand
In the syncline reverberation
Of new burgeoned night

I climb from the constraint
Of argon lights
As if this raddled orange stain
Were a final, civilising sphere of influence
An emissary of the grace-full sun
The dark a tendril crawling
When I open up to shout

The band, of course, plays on

In the apocalypse
Days pass like distant birds
We do not exactly know what kind
Only that, from here their flight is slow
On the wall, crocodile hands enfold
I suppose, for my amusement
Another hungry prayer
Somewhere outside
A car rumbles in the clumsy quiet
Maybe Wednesday, maybe autumn
We sojourn at home
As if marooned in a now contemptuous land
The trees still harbour spring
We sometimes shake like leafs
Tremulous and tentatively attached
Courting déjà vus like raw easterlies
At least, for now, the kettle groans
A familiar, urgent groan
Its weight not quite as comforting
As it used to be

The congregation for the causes of the saints
Are watching for new miracles
Who is dead and by what ruse, arisen

On Hart Island prisoners
Lay out whitewashed boxes
In neat rows like cockleshells

In machine cut trenches
Marine ply layered over
So the worm beneath the sea won't grow

Pumping from the pit a kind of slurry
Admixtured with entreatied earth
As the laden dead displace their cells

The way neglectful tears
Instil an oiled gleam
Look up, shout Eureka
The sky all glamoured
A brassed coin
Ridden, misered, free

When warders solemn and contrary
Ringing vagrant bells
Bow low to chain the ankles
Of the escapading dead

You can only walk so far on water
Til the Rikers Island ferry
With your feet of burden clay
To the potter's field
Calls you home again

We will invest in crematory rites
Plague masks, Netflix and the scritch
    -scratching
Of pencils blunted on hard truths

We are the merry, we are the dead
A bellbird's raucous crying
Here comes a chopper
To chop off your head

I will give you sunsets
Of stained glass broken
At cemetery gates
Chimneys bent like churches
The smoke of charnel dawns
A cross on every second door
To mark where rats
In haute couture are feasting

In Pasadena Christ's spectre has returned
Full of wrath and burning
Truckstops to the ground
Wrapped in grotesques of ink and leather

Sometimes, Sunday
Christmas quiet, the trees are singing
   London Bridge
and Ring-a-ring-a-rosey
I expect the furniture would change
Become dysmorphic and diseased

In rooms by emptiness made small

Instead it sat there smug and somehow
   out of place
Casting a cage of shadows in the corner

The gilded relics of a forgotten age

The perspectives all but bare, the shapes
   burning
In the mendacity of our caustic afterthought

A seeping glow
Where our poised faces once were hung

Now ovals and oblongs
Resonant with a dull departure

As if, in this imago a transformation
The ladder back spread long across the wall
In the arch contradiction of cascade

Now, companioned by watchful birds
In humanless silence

We, the heavens all command
Obeisant
   as the sun

Bowing for our solitary convenience
Staying, all but the same, in the truths
   it derides
(I tell the fleeing crow), is quite ruthless

Grown warier still
As if the people, we carefully avoid
Step brusque, crow cautious
Almost alarmed, wore an unseen face
So much more imposing than the self,
   disguised
I can see the sharp bird beak and bulbous
   eyes
The metal shriek of coins

I take my supplies and coughing, almost run
An innocuous white van
Tinted windows, For Your Health
   marked on the doors
Below a sceptred crown, the beasts, apart
But inevitably crashing, as if borders
   were now a flimsy thing
Borne not by maps and invasive histories
But inside
The space demarcated by a breath

No birds these, but alien in descent
Disposal men in coroner's gloves
The bright impassive anonymity
   of decontamination

Climbing out with taser and syringe
And that long mechanical noose
For catching apes and rabid dogs

—Your wife reported you – get in

I drop the bag of eggs and milk, and think
She will miss the pancakes
I always forget to make

But in the metal hulk
There she is
Masked and gloved and turned away
Eyes wet and disinfectant blue
Mouth tremulous, chagrined

Sorry, my love, I said
I forgot the strawberries
They were out of bread

And with those bags
On your feet and hands
You look like Punchinello
Or possibly you're dead

A crowcraw, muffled threat
Shut up, stupid man
The door closed with a stagey, final clang

A moment's passage, head bent heavier
Than the weight of evening
The trees fall sideways
Through a fallow dusk
Thrown Sunday river horses
A hand on humbled neck
That novel familiar ache
A precursored cold
Glass intermittently breathing
Through these again unmade
Opaque semblances of life
Corner ghosts and watching
An unspectacular sunset
Above the drab efflorescence
Of city's passing silhouette

River Times

Sunday, January 2, 2022

New Corona Strain Reported

02/01/22, Cardiff— Medical authorities in Wales report what may be a new resurgence of the Corona virus. Chief Medical Officer at Powys Health, Anton Singh, has said, "This appears to be a mutated strain, both more virulent and deadly. Marked in some by influenza-like symptoms, while others remain asymptomatic, except for a tendency to speak in a kind of word salad, a phenomenon more often seen in hebephrenia, and some forms of late stage dementia. Our virologists and neurologists have found that the virus resides in the fatty tissues of particular areas of the brain, interfering with the process by which linguistic messages are formed. In most cases, after the onset of the gibberish stage, we have observed a rapid decline towards a haemorrhagic death." When asked if enough was being done to contain this new outbreak, tentatively named Corona-22, Gordon Radovic, Regional Assistant to the Deputy Health Minister, quipped, "Vaccines and intravenous immunoglobin treatments are being developed. What more would you like see done, appoint Dylan Thomas?" NHS staff and first responders have reportedly, in private at least, taken to calling this strain, "The Poet's Affliction".

We cow compliance
Our particular grandeur
Through impassive walls, hung in innocuities
Outshone by nightscapes, and by damask
    curtains
Sounds at first impinge, then become symphonic
The air conditioner re-cycles
The Spectred Crown (as we now call it)
Once had more stars than it deserved
Built for a smaller humanity than we
A familial name exchange
For a flotsam
    designation
The monogram still a cursive stain
On wearied sheets and pillow cases
Worn with a hint of shroud-like apperception
Veni vidi vici
A verbena scent
None come here now, to praise Caesar
But to depose
Not long ago, I could tell you
How the mean curve of iridium sales
Would give portent of satellites
    and heart attacks
Now, I could not say
If the greying morning
Means the sun will rise

Caesar, Sybil says, in the purblind dark
The TV mutter, redly glowing
Tell me what this trap means
This graph that charts the half-life
Of poetic utterances
To the decay of meaning
And in fine sibilance, a hissing kind of death
More cursory than cursive
—You can see why it caught
   my frissoned attention

I suppose as sense dismays
When we no longer understand it
(Sotto voce)
Full of light and silence
We become a kind of catatonic
As if the gain had been turned up
All that remains, the loudness of the universe
A darkly kind of death
— With no hope?
With no hope —
I cannot tell you

The hotel staff in masks and plastic suits
Eyes weary and translucent
Leave us trays of ready meals
Bland and impotent
When they deign to speak
With that peculiar rigour of ordinary voices
(Wary of an appearance
   of rhythm, rhyme or reason)
Still call us guests or detainees (by mistake)
Not obsequious employees, in crooked hat
Hand demeaning for a tip
But dour public servants, with that insipid
   hate
Of we few unlegalled prisoners
With that resent (perhaps)
That they are prisoned too

Caesar Seetham, Doctor Mowbray at half seven
One says through the half cracked door
(As if time still had compulsion
   or any urgency)
With that inscrutable reluctance
As if in deathhouse nonchalance
Inviting me to fulfil
A swan song in an electric chair

The corridors spiral in their way
My costumed guard clearing a path
   with a sounding bell
In a peculiar kind of play
Half quarter back, half leper,
   I advance towards the goal

The doctor's rooms, incongruously newly white
Crowded with insect machinery,
   the hotel paintings
Bland as manicured evergreens, hung back
   on the walls

— Seetham
— Mowbray
How are we progressing (he has
   a serpentine sibilance)
In his discomfiting rhetoric
As if a cobra mouth behind the mask
Spat disarming blandishments
Do you have much news of the world
—None I can relay
Silence, in the susurrus, is sharp as needles
We have a new kind of test
An isotope that will trace
The paths and disinclinations
Of the proteins and disinhibitors

The virus in its devices
    and manufactories has marked
We hope to see if it's shaping can be unshaped
—And if I say No?
—No?
—No

-**No.**

—Nothing then for the ringing in my ears?
Sometimes in the silence it has an unseemly
    voice.
—What's it say?
Ah that my friend is the question I never hope
    to ask
Sleeve up, lie down, anaesthetic in the arm
The dye goes in the neck

— I never doubted it.

You know these rooms are much too small
For the living or the dead
I tell Sybil, playing hangman in her breath
She is pressed against the nightside window,
    sighing
The lights are like the sea, she says
Where we met, you know, the fateful day – ha ha
Though that word is not quite correct
Just call it star-crossed
The hollow bottles echoing
On the sea wall where you arranged them
A fate full tune and the coloured light
Diminishing far across the water
–I could not see you
With the sun behind
Only that familiar shape
The way I see you now
The evening passing through
To a benign horizon
Look!

Like birds, they're fighting
Whiplash trolls in safety vests
Scarves like wolves
Slung about their mouths and necks
All worldly goods contrived in ricket-wheeled
    and wire inconveniences

Grave and desperate as untethered astronauts
Beating swollen motion for a breath

— Is that a child, that they have?
She asks urgent, against the glass
A tremored mist dissolves to black
As a van pulls up
In that fearful and nondescript ubiquity
Suddenly they stop and all look
Perhaps like lambs suspecting eagles
In the flickered blackout, all goes dark
When the light recalls
The haphazard street
Everyone is gone
Leaving, on the pavement
Just a windswept tangle
Of yellow knotted string

In the refectory morning
We gather carefully apart
A necessary socialization
So the plague birds can pretend concern
For our mental health
In the corner, he has a zealot eye
A snail shell, a saviour aspect
More martyr than savoir faire
She says, with a rolling eye
A rorschach blackness dawning
Askance as he declares
– It is the end of days
We have three riders
And just await a fourth
A woman riding by, her enduring pestilence
Neither living, nor the dead
But half-lifed
(He takes an egg in hand)
This is the embryonic world
Albumen below a fragile shell
The germ a new born sun
There is more in heaven
Than we dare
The earth has shed her skin and left us here
Bewildered in the dross
Imagining this translucence something holy

In the air I smell that dry serpent stench
He shells and swallows, the ovoid almost whole
With an ugly movement in his throat
Repulsive vermin, Sybil says
Eyes still gleaming
While I fetch new buttered bread from the buffet
She approaches where he and his disciples play
All atangled
As if this were any ordinary day
— I was once a young jongluer, he says
Now a lord in waiting
I suspected you were once a fool, she rejoins
Unsheathing
A lipstick to her mouth
She presses a napkin to her lips
I will give you this (she casts the fabric
   at his feet)
When this is done, come claim it

There is always half a melon
On the platter, like John the Baptist's head
Untouched, but the honey slowly bleeding
In the centre and on the edge
So when I cast it down (but soft)
A locust cornucopia
To the mosaic anagrams, it broke apart and lay
Like the pulped remains

Of an enormous slug
Through the swinging doors a stranger comes
Locust-eyed
Wrapped in hazard tape and plastic
Grown large the way a beast in warning does
Raving that the world still makes small sense
This is necessarily a temporary happenstance
Stay calm, soon all will return
With market fluctuations and fashionable
    lapels
And the extraordinary visions
Of prescient door bells
A world still fit for gamesmen
Pennants flying at the goal
A blue as blue as heroes
That the hoipolloi may never touch
Here, at the Baptist s feet, the stranger fell
A slime rolling from his skin and draggled hair
— My mouth! My mouth! The Baptist cried
— The filth went in
He clamped a fist against his lips
As if, denying egress, he could somehow prevail
While pestilence bloomed inside
As all acolytes ricocheted around him
The hazmat guards came in
Dragged the limp (dead?) wild man
And as the Baptist wept, led him too,
    to a dusky death

You are medjool sweet, my love
I torn as Casablanca
A warfare kind of envy
– At least they may cut off his liar's head
To search out stars like diamonds
In the saffron red

– As the autumn leaves, I am only flirting
It is boring here, I have not fell
You are deathly dull, always rhyming
I am more inclement, cool but not contrite

Do you not know that in a time
When our borders close
Those within from those without
This intimate radiance
Is the greater threat
How then do we trust
A hand foregone, that I have never reached?

– Now I am reaching

But soft, I hear a harmony
The sun augurs, through the morning silt
Of oneway glass

Doctor Mowbray in the door, robed and masked
A peculiar ventriloquary
As if he spoke from some outre relic
Of the monochromatic dead

– You will know, perhaps
How a bird, in that complex of trills and larks
Sings out its unique name
To mark a kind of invisible terrain
To teach, to know
Its hatchlings from all the rest
An ape too, has a song, crooning to itself
In its sweet, anticipatory joys
For a favourite, gathered feast,
   or the familiar in the face of love
We uniquely, join these two
A song a kind of thought
Defining the area that is the other
   and the self
Imbued with joy
Now imagine this in disarray, a babble
   if you will
Of commingled voices, foregoing love and joy
   and reason
For this disjointed patternation
The self unhinged becomes the size of the world
That does not recall its face

You go on, Caesar, that is your key
Perhaps your Rubicon
When others have failed, found a hideous silence
Unmouthed and comatose
After their brief protestation
Of vociferous grandiloquence
You go on, almost making sense
We have determined, a protein in your blood
Bound up in haemoglobulin
Extracted and transfused
May bring those who have succumbed
Back from the faceless quiet
At the end of wrecksome utterances
A carotid applause
We will have you, bringing out of silence
All recitations numb
As if by egress you swallowed up the world
The way of monstrous insects

So, much is given to allay the irksome moment
And, alas, so much still withheld
Ere the sun forgives the morning
I will see the night
You will not have my blood

I think your cotton dress
With the daisies on
Smells like freshly ironed summer
Heads all strangely solemn

—I have left that far behind
Now only this disinfectant scent
On my hands and cheek
God still demands that I get my new coiffure
But I will forego all such constraints
For

Today the sun is green
As the scarf across your face
I think the earth resents
Our furore, and would cast us off
Ringing bells, muttering, sotto voce
Unclean, unclean
Forgive our sprawling miasma
For a kinder silence
Relinquish all such meaning
Out of Eden
For a flight
We do not forgive ourselves

Teenage vampires in Rome
Have ousted all the priests
Blood and Ozymandias on their lips
Aeroplanes dismay the air
Screaming out the sky is changing
In a roar of smoke and molten wings

—I have grown so strangely light
Keeping all such declarations within
I suppose it is counterintuitive
With nothing left to say
It is in their exculpation we grow weight

Perhaps you sleep
Perhaps a ceaseless voice
A kind, indelible fire
Almost, perhaps, a whisper
I think I hear the crowcraw
In your throat

The rooms are much too small
I don't think they can bear my weight
A noise suffuses like the surface of the sun
Sovereignly she floats upwards
As if she were a kite, released and with a spasm
Catching temeritous winds
Flaunt a gallows
I had thought to reach
As she slunk through the transom
Arms lax at her sides
A smile, confusion, bliss
On her upturned face

My thought somehow truncated
The action it commanded half undone
My fingers closing short
Of the threadbare hem
I remembered how her jeans
Had daisies embroidered on
Long tattered and unpicked
Until
Just the darker silhouette remained

There is a bitter bark

    Under shreds, exposed

        I am chlorine green

A nasal, summer drone

A noisome heat

        Mercurochrome

Stained through in pestilent sunshine

    Cicada loosing skin
      Discarding empty life

      Grown too small and blind
The husks of half-persistent dreams

In fierce inalienable determination

I think;
You were the tree
I clung to

The Weeken

Saturday, February 29, 2020

New Threat To Aviation

29/02/22. There have been unconfirmed reports that a woman seen floating above a Corona Hotel in an undisclosed part of the city was shot down by An F18 fighter jet last night. Decontamination Units were seen scrambling. The Minister for Aviation has said that there is no new threat to aviation. Meanwhile reports of similar incidents around the world of what is being called "gravitational annulment" have also been dismissed As ridiculous by scientists and government spokespeople. There are reports that people in China are wearing weights When outdoors, though, given the strangeness of the phenomena, there is some doubt as to whether that will be effective. Others are wearing string, rope, and in one community by the coastal village of Hachijo, Japan, even fishing lines as tethers. The people of Hachijojima, seen floating over the popular fishing spots and beaches, have in local reports been dubbed, The Fish Kite Folk.

I have loved you like the plague
In our terrarium seclusion
Decaying and renewed
In an alien homeostasis
As if a small green world
Harboured everything you need

A crow from the sea
I will take an axe in hand
With all constituent anxieties

To dismember doors and fallen trees
As if in pieces
All that companion and circumspect
    significance gone
Poured away like evening's laughter

The sun wears a crown
Here we are still tangled in her shine
Spilling to the street
Swept by cattle stink
In that eighteen wheeler, death
Is not abattoir discrete
But a sting, the cast grit
A scintillation in the eye
How this astigmatism, stretched
At the wounded corner weeps

Caesar
       You weight
Regrets like gold
As if the sun bled out
Not quite dying
By a turnbuckle sea
Repulsing all attempts at rescue
Holding me in impassive inclinations
Your grip a mantis love
Drowning both of us
In the fevered roar
Deaf as seashells
My tenterhooks as distanced
As a saviour

When she left, I fled and burnt the note

Outside, I thought I heard
For the first time today
A kind of bird, maybe nondescript
But singing out its name
With the insistent declaration
Of an almost empty world
A green shoot writhing
Up from the earth
Neither challenge nor defiance
Just finding in the interstices

The necessity of life

Today I found a word
In a poem, like a welt
I forgot, a winter sting
Fragile and jarring
As spiderwebs on tricycle spokes
Prodigies, to stop the wheel
In dove trepidation
A hand brave in the wheel
Slowly turning
Loud as people
Shaking butterflies
From neon burning buildings
Raising fists like bridges
Forsaking carnival laughter
For breathless homilies
Not yet done with drowning
In prison they gave us guitars
With broken frets, and for our safety
Kneeling, on my neck and back
Without strings

Night swells from diminished day
So we go around again

We have no face at pigstock
Except this heat wet mask
We cattle them in their stink
Breathing, breathing, breathing
A hard roar as we shift

On Butterfly Street
The buildings watch
With bright impassive windows
Blind taped against the riot
Crosses on their eyes and on their mouths

You know they are just diurnal moths
A pig mask says, venom dripping
All summer, without hearts
On either side of the island
That with gauzy indifference
Neat divides the road

They crack their perspex shields
With fierce new beats press on

Today, no ears
I will not pretend
Jesus saves tall buildings
In the crucible descent
Of grit and cortisone fire escapes
We are the windblown dead
Leaves crumpled, umbered, swept
From any stray proscenium
Where stratagems display
A fine disregard
For the changing seasons
An armillary
In your smile
Some half-formed days the sky still bleeds
    haphazard stars
Our ignorance so great
The world again fragments
In virulence and babble
At the cenotaph
They gather with the dead
Not to choose a different day
But in return, to glory

Do you have a dollar, do you have a light
I am blind, you can see
The scars like butterflies
That's what my mother said
When I got back, though I was proud to fight
— I'm sorry, no
It's very quiet, in the dawn, I heard
A hoofed creature, I am certain
It walked right up I felt its nose
Velvet soft, you see the blood? Harry?
Harry, you see the blood?
On Hare Island we killed them all
You with your ten-eighty smile
I in my chlorphosphate silence
The rabbits and the wild cats
The foxes with bright midnight howls
The staggerers under disco lights
The mutterers in filthy streets
C4 and submachine guns and the gas
If it doesn't make them cry and run, ignites
With that soft whoosh of butterflies
The only question that remained
Is with life extinguished, this island's name
Makes little sense
I think we will make a world

Of barbaric contour lines
Zones of egress, nameless
A terrain without a map
Fit for warriors, and in
Their passing silence, shapes
The vaingloried silhouette
Of butterflies
Do you have a dollar
Do you have a light?

But seeing the van coming
The blind soldier rifle bent
Twitching in his furies and laments
I his humbug coat

And fled

When the morning sun
Jags and buckles a new horizon
Crooked chimneys plume
An ephemeral garniture
Windows in new sunlight break
A creak of knuckled blinds
The last storm-calm of night dispels
Shadows shadow long
A man in his shabby borrowed coat
Draws the midriff tight
To keep the crow warm in his chest
Leashed in bird-black laughter

— Seetham
Mowbray
— We have you back
Perhaps

But I find

My philosophy does not reside
In your high and long and laboured art
But discerns a moment's escape
In the ecstatic griffonage
Of my mellifluous glossolalia

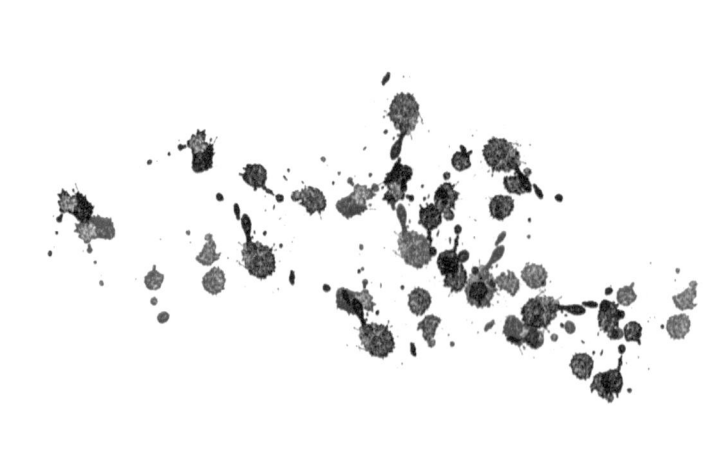

I thought, a bird

or the gilded sun

which, I do not know

only that it sung

with a voice of fire

of drowning days

of a neglectful re-emergence

the beach almost as long

as this piece of forever

the way the sea-wrack turns

with gull consolations

the spatter sands in rivulet devils runs

the winter breaks, in capitulation

a kind of lightning, raked from oblate stone

a muttered sigil for imprisoned time

that you skipped away

That one has a bird

— see it flying

                                        (you said)

half a breath, pointing to the eye

inflected in the spill of sun

a hard and dead and watchful kind of god

in the yellow, a threat of blood

moaning in the threadbare winds

that shawl a solace from

the haze of evening

if you scorn her, listening

how she swells

a song, a eulogy, a tide

a glare as wary as a loss

wings tilted

in obeisant reclamation

We have found
In those honeyed and predatory times
Gone like the winter sun
Poetry an affliction
Now we find a kind of tincture
Extracted and sublimed
From the blood of poets
Will make us strong
This is a farm
Not as you surmise
A sanatorium
In the throes of your resistance
The vitality that sings
Is also undermined
By a chimeric alteration
Of the humours, of the spin
Of the autonomous delight
Of that molecule we have aptly named
Haphazard Grace
For it to be efficacious
You must bow
Open up a vein and give in

− Tell me then of the world
I may be leaving

In Wisconsin, semi-autos in their teeth
A thousand patriot martyrs died
Spouting liberty or death
Choosing, I suppose, the latter
Still, quite perplexed
Port au Prince is burning
Jerusalem is beneath an Easter pall
The crucifixions something to behold
In New York (those left alive)
Are living underground
Rat kings rule the surface
Tails intertwined
Hong Kong is lost below
A turning octopus sea
In Africa they have crowned a locust king
God is not a vaccine
From such flimsy towers we are leaping
The president claps along
Singing one-a-penny
   and other children's songs
Wolves hunt us in the streets
We hunt them
In glorious abdications
Mammoths walk the steppes
(Escaped from a Wuhan lab
In striking irony)

In unexpected quietude
The world begun to cool
A few litres of your blood
An unimmaculate territory
Could see at last an end to all of this

— At last at least
And if I will not give it up?

We will not take it

— And still, noblesse oblige
If I will not give it up?
W
e will not take it

— And still
Though kings and paupers fall?

We will not take it

And if she falls?

(Chorus) — We will not take it

Why my blood, it is not particularly rare
   or fine
Just the common muck
Mixed up with history's brute vagaries
Fathered from uncounted shores
Mothered in short kindness
Adulterated by all the whims and follies
Of indulgent fortune

– Caesar, it is simply this
Of seven and seven billion souls
Each that makes this fast descent
In a score or month or se'night
Finding only,
A sparse and dirigible nonsense
Coma, oblivion, death
Yet you ramble on, for months
In peculiar disinclination
You still make a kind of sense

(Chorus) – We must take it!

You will not find me
In broken mirrors
Shedding piecemeal reflections
Now
Dancing for a new day of the dead

Imagine a world
With only poets left alive
Burying the many lost
In eulogies and faded roses
Tractor slow
Cutting furrows
Through the brow of heaven
And the face of our imagined hells
Frenetically dying
At each sunfall
Only in the unexpected rise
To dance St Thomas's dance again

Calcium is made in stars
Therefore the infinite bones
Of the universe are wide
We are but one efflorescence
From the god reaction
Of a crystal turned to seed
To mar the surface
Of a minuet
Until this uncertain craquelure
Breaks in exposure
This last retort

After the cull
(If this works)
While we resound
Like apes and birds
We will fight and scream
Bury and lament the dead
Extolling our mythopoeic imperatives
But if there are only poets left alive
Who in hell will do the washing up?

About the Author

C S Hughes grew up in ochre towns and cerulean cities. He has worked as a spice seller, a book dealer and a watch fixer. He has had poetry and stories published in print and online journals, including Newtown News, Five 2 One, Blue Pepper, The Blue Nib, Weird Tales and others.

He has released several collections of poetry, including The Book Of Whimsies, The Book Of Barbarous Tales, The Little Book Of Funerals and The Book Of Bird & Bear.

He edited and published two very successful collections – The Poetry Of John-Ashdown Hill, and From The Ashes – Poetry In Support of the 2019-2020 Australian Bushfire Relief Effort.

He is currently safely ensconced with a cat and an historian in the cool, green hills in the south eastern part of Australia.

Synops

Caesar Seetham, former financial consultant and erstwhile poet, is reported by his mercurial wife Sybil for breaching home quarantine, as a new, mutated strain of coronavirus sweeps the world. To her chagrin, she finds herself confined with him in the close quarters of The Sceptred Crown – a third rate corona hotel. While chaos reigns in the outside world, strange new symptoms emerge. Those infected with COVID-22 show few symptoms at first, except a tendency to gibber and babble in a kind of deranged and semi-poetic aphasia, before rapidly succumbing to silence, coma, haemorrhage and death.

While Caesar records his impressions of a world gone mad, Dr Mowbray, in charge at the Sceptred Crown, learns that a unique antibody in Caesar's blood could prevent the progress of the disease, leaving the infected, like Caesar, although trapped in a state of poetic aphasia, at least not declining into coma and death. For the process to succeed, Caesar must not only calmly and willingly give up his blood, but he must submit to having every drop drained, also giving up his life – the only way Mowbray will be able to extract enough antibodies to create a viable serum.

While Caesar considers what his life is worth, Sybil is struck by even more disturbing symptoms, and if he can't even save the woman he <u>loves, why the hell should he bother saving the world?</u>

www.ingramcontent.com/pod-product-compliance
Lightning Source LLC
Chambersburg PA
CBHW020329010526
44107CB00054B/2032